OCARINA

Pooya Jamalian

Copyright

INTRODUCTION

Introduction for students

The origin of the ceramic pipe goes back to an ancient civilization of the 3rd and 4th centuries BC. At that time, the pipes had fewer holes, some of them had only 3 or 4 scales, or people just breathed into the pot-shaped pipes.

The ceramic pipe that we see now has existed since the middle of the 19th century. The original form was born in a small town in northern Italy. From its form the derivation of the word ocarina is said to be "small goose". The Tyrolean poets praised it throughout Europe. Simple and familiar with the fulfilling depth of a beautiful sound, the ocarina was appreciated by all sorts of people and soon gained popularity in Europe, from which it spread all over the world.

The ocarina boom passed over Japan without it being much noticed. By producing music for the NHK program "The Great Yellow River" in 1986, the sound of the ocarina prevailed all over Japan. Now, the population of ocarina lovers is increasing in Japan, and most of them have been influenced by Sojiro's music.

Hint for Ocarina Players

We Have Online Courses for Ocarina Players from Beginner to Advanced. If you want to Learn & Register in Classes as Professional Player, Please Contact Us.

Whatsapp Number: +989393699242

Mail: pooya.woodwind@yahoo.com

Our Social Media:

pooya.jamalian

lakotaflute

Twelve Hole
Ocarina Fingering Chart

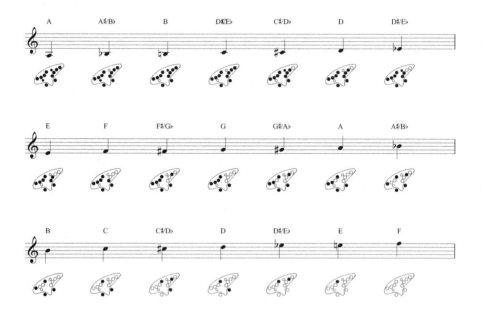

SECTION 1
Warm Up

WARM UP 1

ШАRM UP 2

4

7

9

Ocarina

WARM UP 3

WARM UP 4

Ocarina

WARM UP 5

ШARM UP 6

Ocarina

WARM UP 7

ШARM UP 8

Ocarina

WARM UP 9

ШARM UP 10

Ocarina

WARM UP 11

WARM UP 12

Ocarina

WARM UP 13

SECTION 2

Lessons

1. GHOGHAYE SETAREGAN

Teaching points:

Every note begins with an articulation, except when we play slurred (legato).

Single tonguing:
The T articulation closes the gate for the airstream, momentarily cutting off the sound. It' s executed with the very
tip of the tongue.

Ocarina

2. GOLUMCAN

Teaching points:

Tie:

When tied together,two notes with the same pitch are played as a single note.

The length of this single note is the sum of the time values of the two tied notes.

3. CAN'T HELP FALLING IN LOVE

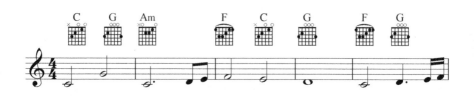

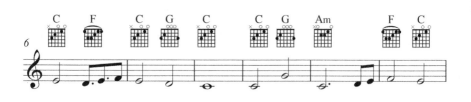

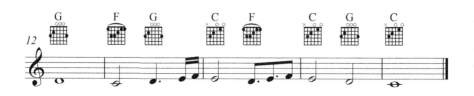

Teaching points:

Rhythmic values of notes:

Note	Beats	Note	Beats
𝅝	4 beats	𝅝 .	6 beats
𝅗𝅥	2 beats	𝅗𝅥 .	3 beats
♩	1 beat	♩ .	1½ beats
♪	½ beat	♪ .	¾ beat

4. JOMEH (FARHAD)

Teaching points:

Time signatures indicate the number of beats in each measure
(the top number)
and also show what type of note represents a single beat
(the bottom number).

Simple time signatures Such as:
4/4,3/4,2/2,2/4,... .

Compound time signatures such as:
6/8

5. CARAVANSARY (KITARO)

Teaching points:

You have to play F notes as F sharp (#) in this lesson.

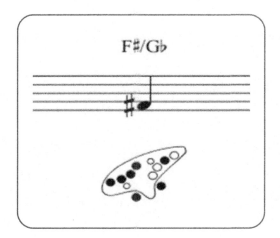

F#/G♭

Ocarina

6. BELLA CIAO

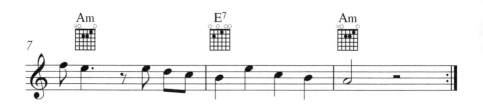

Teaching points:

Rhythmic values of rests:

Whole rest Semibreve rest	1	▬	
Half rest Minim rest	1/2	▬	
Quarter rest Crotchet rest	1/4		
Eighth rest Quaver rest	1/8		
Sixteenth rest Semiquaver rest	1/16		
Thirty-second rest Demisemiquaver rest	1/32		
Sixty-fourth rest Hemidemisemiquaver rest	1/64		

7. SCARBOROUGH FAIR

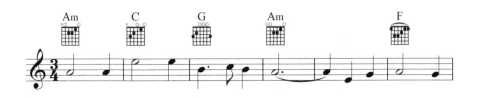

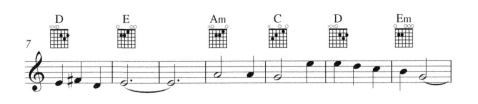

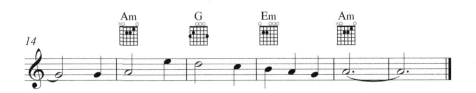

Teaching points:

Attention to time signature in this lesson (3/4).

8. CITY STARS

Teaching points:

A Tuplet is a group of notes that wound not normally fit into the rhythmic space they occupy.
The example shown is a quarter-note triplet-three quarter notes are to be played in the space that would normally contain two.

Ocarina

9. A TIME FOR US

Teaching points:

Sonority is another word for timbre. The timbre or sonority of an instrument or voice is the colors, character or quality of sound it produces.
It is so important for player to have sonority while playing instrument.

10. NEFRIN (ARTOUSH)

Teaching points:

Use ornaments techniques while playing.

ornamentation, in music, the embellishment of a melody, either by adding notes or by modifying rhythms. In European music, ornamentation is added to an already complete composition in order to make it more pleasing.

11. SADNESS AND SORROW

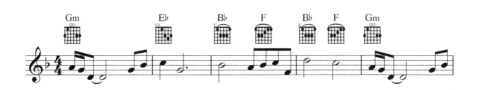

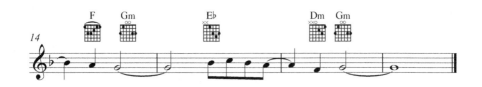

Teaching points:

You have to play B notes as B flat (b) in this lesson.

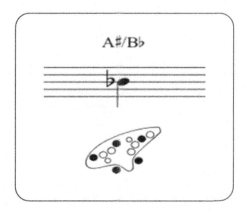

12. DONA DONA

Teaching points:

Repeat part of the lesson that you have trouble with it again and again to improve that.

Ocarina

13. FAIRY FOOTSTEP IN GREENLAND

Teaching points:

You have to play B notes as B flat (b) in this lesson.

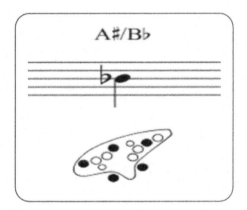

14. ABR MIBARAD
(HOMAYOUN SHAJARIAN)

Teaching points:

A beautiful Persian song and melody, sang by Homayoun Shajarian who is famous as
a great artist in the world.

Ocarina

15. FLY ME TO THE MOON

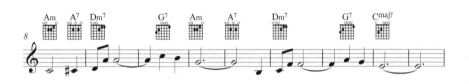

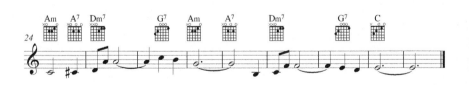

Teaching points:

You have to use this fingering to play G sharp (#) and C sharp (#).

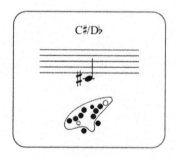

16. IN AKHARIN BARE (E31)

Teaching points:

Legato is the slurring of a number of notes in one uninterrupted stream of air, without articulating each note. It can be a great tool to work on use of air, and on
the coordination between different fingerings. If the notes are not separated by articulation, this exposes all of the imperfections of unevenly moving fingers.

Ocarina

17. LONELY SHEPHERD

Teaching points:

"The Lonely Shepherd" is an instrumental piece by James Last, first released in a recording with the Romanian Panflutist Gheorghe Zamfir.

18. MY HEART WILL GO ON

Teaching points:

Staccato notes are separated from each other by playing each note as short as possible. The breath support remains active all the time, and the tongue makes the difference: instead of Tu, we say a very short Tu(t), the latter (t) being silent, with the tip of the tongue against the palate. Portato is everything in the middle, from almost slurred but articulated, to a slightly broader
version than staccato.

19. TEARS IN HEAVEN

Ocarina

Teaching points:

"Tears in Heaven" is a song by Eric Clapton and Will Jennings, written about the death of Clapton's four-year-old son.

On 20 March 1991, Clapton's 4-year-old son Conor died after falling from the 53rd-floor window of a New York City apartment.

Ocarina

20. THE LAST OF US

Teaching points:

"The Last of Us" is a 2013 action-adventure game developed by Naughty Dog
and published by Sony Computer Entertainment.

The original score was composed and performed by Gustavo Santaolalla.

21. GAME OF THRONES

Teaching points:

You have to play B notes as B flat (b) in this lesson.

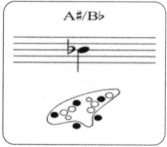

And to use F sharp (#) use:

Ocarina

22. SPIRIT AWAY

Teaching points:

You have to play F notes as F sharp (#) in this lesson.

Ocarina

23. THEME OF LOVE
(FINAL FANTASY IV)

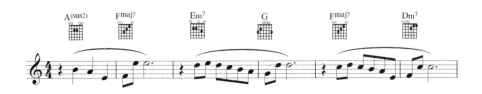

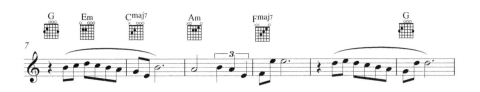

Teaching points:

To observe:
Legato and Tuplet in this lesson.

24. A POEM OF REVIVIFICATION (SOJIRO)

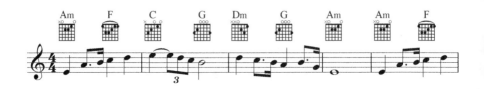

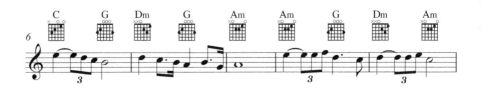

Teaching points:

One of the beautiful songs of Master Sojiro with different arrangement by me.

Ocarina

25.YESTERDAY-BEATLES

Teaching points:

"Yesterday" is a song by the English rock band the Beatles, written by Paul McCartney and credited to Lennon–McCartney.

It was first released on the album Help! in August 1965, except in the United States, where it was issued as a single in September.

The song reached number one on the US charts. It subsequently appeared on the UK EP Yesterday in March 1966 and made its US album debut on Yesterday and Today, in June 1966.

"And I will be immensely grateful if you post a Reader Review on the book's product page at the online bookstore where you purchased it. These reviews are an essential resource, and it's sad but true that readers of books seldom bother to post their comments, good or bad! You can also make suggestions in the course of writing a review. Believe me, I read them all. Thank you! – Pooya Jamalian"

Another Book: Lakota Flute

Copyright

Author name: Seyyed Pooya Jamalian
Author address: Unit 5 , 2nd floor, Morvarid Tower, Morvarid St, 10th Nasim St, Koohk St, Chitgar, Tehran, Iran
ISBN: 9798408885794 (Paperback)
Cover designer name: Mohammad Mahdi Ghafoori Kaffash
Layout designer name: Mohammad Mahdi Ghafoori Kaffash
www.irantoamazon.com
First printing edition 2022.

CONTENTS

Printed in Great Britain
by Amazon

39075060R00046